MW01049089

LARRY BURKETT

SURVIVING THE 90'S ECONOMY

MOODY PRESS

CHICAGO

© 1992 by
CHRISTIAN FINANCIAL CONCEPTS

The material in this book has been compiled from *The Coming Economic Earthquake* by Larry Burkett.

All Scripture quotations, unless noted otherwise, are from the *New American Standard Bible,* © 1960, 1962, 1963, 1968, 1971, 1972, 1973, 1975, and 1977 by The Lockman Foundation, and are used by permission.

ISBN: 0-8024-2609-3

3 5 7 9 10 8 6 4 2

Printed in the United States of America

About the Author

Larry Burkett is committed to teaching God's people His principles for managing money. Unfortunately, money management is one area often neglected by Christians, and it is a major cause of conflict and disruption in both business and family life.

For more than two decades Larry has counseled and taught God's principles for finance across the country. As president of Christian Financial Concepts, Larry has counseled, conducted seminars, and written numerous books on the subject of maintaining control of the budget. In additon he is heard on more than 1,000 radio outlets worldwide.

Introduction

Allen and Kathy had planned for their new home a long while. Both of them had good jobs with stable companies and knew they could well afford the payments. So, with more than a little trepidation, they signed the papers committing to the construction loan. That was in September of 1990.

Kathy was excited to see the progress of the "dream" home. First the lot was cleared; then the foundation laid. Within two months the walls were going up and their home was beginning to look like a real home.

As 1991 began, Allen became visibly nervous about the state of the economy. He was a systems analyst with a well-established software firm and had never experienced even a minor slowdown in demand for his services. Suddenly, he saw three of his major clients back out of pending jobs and, for the first time ever, found himself with excess time on his hands. Rumors of pending layoffs were flying throughout the company. Allen discounted most of them as just that: rumors.

A year earlier he had turned down two of his clients who had offered him sizable bonuses to leave his company and come to work for them. It was the benefits package offered by his company that made him decide to stay where he was. So although the company might be experiencing some short-term setbacks, Allen was sure his position was secure. But with so much negative talk in the company and all their savings plus another $100,000 going into a new home, he had something of a queasy feeling inside.

Then in July the company announced that for the first time in history they would be reducing their labor force through involuntary cutbacks. Even as the division manager was speaking, it still didn't really register with Allen. *Involuntary cutbacks*, he thought silently, trying to focus on what that meant to him: *layoffs! That is what the manager was saying.*

Introduction

Allen's mind refocused just as he heard the manager say, "We have decided to phase out our involvement in the multi-user system in order to concentrate on our primary area of operations: the single-user personal computer system. All personnel involved in multi-user design and operation will be given thirty days notice, effective today."

The words hit Allen like a lightening bolt out of a clear sky! He was the senior analyst in the multi-user department and had logically assumed that all others would be released before he would. Now he was faced with the worst case scenario: the entire department would be eliminated.

The next two months were the worst in Allen and Kathy's lives. Allen's job, as well as that of twenty others, was eliminated with no more regard for his personal situation than if he had been a part-time worker from some temp-service agency. His five years of dedicated service to the company seemed to mean nothing to the senior management. Later he read in the trade journals that the company was in a desperate condition because of overexpansion and too much high interest debt. The company president was released, although his "golden parachute" eased his problems with a million dollar severance package.

Allen was not so fortunate. "What will we do?" Kathy said softly, trying not to show the distress she was feeling. She knew Allen had all the pressure he could take. He had written virtually every software company in the three-state area that might remotely be related to his specialty, but to no avail. Companies that were scouting for his services a year earlier closed their doors to him.

Allen was able to generate some income by maintaining programs he had written for previous clients, but at an hourly rate, and without any benefits.

"Kathy, we're just going to have to back out on the house," Allen told his distraught wife. "There's no way we'll be able to get a permanent loan with me out of work. And the payments on the construction loan will eat up my severance pay in two months."

"But we'll lose everything we have put into it so far," Kathy protested. However, inside she wasn't sure that her concern was over the money they had paid as much as it was the loss of the home she had dreamed about.

"Kathy, be realistic," Allen snapped. "I don't want to lose that money either, but I don't have a job and it doesn't look like I'm going to be able to find one at the salary I was making, if at all. Now grow up!"

Kathy was stunned by Allen's outburst, and she broke down crying. "You don't have to blame me," she yelled through the tears she couldn't contain. "I didn't cause this. I'm still working, you know."

The minute she said it she regretted it. The hurt on Allen's face showed immediately. He was out of work and out of hope. In less than six months his entire life had been turned upside down. And instead of planning what furniture they would need for their new home they were living on credit cards and facing lawsuits from the bank and the developer.

Allen and Kathy didn't do anything differently from what millions of other young couples do every day. In a debt-run society almost everyone presumes upon the future to one degree or another. In this young couple's case the economy caught them.

With each passing phase our economy traps more and more families; many are beyond the age where they can recover economically. Understanding how and why our economy cycles is essential to long-term financial success.

THE TRANSFER OF WEALTH

In the early 1980s I was teaching financial conferences around the country and felt compelled by the Lord to share my belief (then and now) that no economy can absorb forever the amount of debt that our economy is experiencing. But most people didn't want generalities. They wanted times and dates, so I was often asked, "How long until the economy collapses?"

At the time, I suggested the longest period I could conceive this huge transfer of wealth would continue— ten years. But ten years have come and gone and the economy still survives. We are deeper in debt than even the most liberal of liberals ever dreamed we would be, and yet we continue to operate in a somewhat "normal" fashion.

The actual deficits are almost twice as large as those admitted by the government. So why hasn't our economy collapsed? Because the American people still have confidence in "the system." The heart of the system depends on borrowing to fund the budget deficits each year. The interest on a $3 trillion debt amounts to $240 billion annually, or about 40 percent of all personal income taxes paid. When this debt swells to $20 trillion in nine years or so, the annual interest will be $1.6 trillion, or about 200 percent of all personal income taxes projected for that year (at a 33 percent rate).

So how do we break out of this debt spiral? We don't. Unfortunately we have no choice but to continue with more of the same.

The "poor" get federal subsidies for education, housing, health care, even food. The wealthy have enough to provide these benefits for themselves. The middle class borrow against the little equity they have remaining to pay for what they need.

We have another "Catch 22" in the transfer of wealth out of our country. As the national debt continues to grow, our dependence on foreign loans continues to mount. Eventually the interest leaving the country will exceed the government's tax revenues. Then a "solution" must be found.

A short-range solution will be more taxes. One recurring suggestion is to tax the "wealthy" more. The difficulty is that if all the income above $100,000 a year were taken from the wealthy, it would operate our government for only ten days! Also, stripping the wealthy of all their surpluses is a little like killing the goose that lays the golden egg. The poor don't invest for the future. They need all they have just to live.

The second part of this Catch 22 is the danger of foreign investors not lending us the money we need. If they stop lending, then we must print the money (monetize the debt). When we begin this process, hyperinflation is certain to follow.

I have concluded that accurately predicting the precise time of a major economic downturn (great depression) is virtually impossible. Furthermore, until we get inside the "window of statistical probability," all attempts to establish a time is purely guesswork. The window of statistical probability occurs when the circumstances get so bad economically that no amount of further manipulation is possible to keep the economy going at a reasonably normal pace. For a more in-depth analysis of why and how the economy will collapse, see my recent book entitled *The Coming Economic Earthquake.*

The Growth of Debt

Americans have mortgaged their futures to buy the homes they have come to expect. Even the recent trend back to smaller, simpler homes has not brought the average home within the income range of the average family. The current median income per family is $36,000 (1991). Based on this income, an average home should sell for approximately $72,000. Instead, it sells for just under $108,000. Those who buy at these prices, and many do, find themselves in constant financial difficulties.

A recent study by the President's Council on the Family showed that if the real value of homes were reflected (what a qualified buyer is willing and able to pay) Americans would have a negative equity in their homes. Less than 2 percent of all Americans own their homes debt-free, and the average length of home mortgages still owed by retirees (sixty-two and older) is twenty-two years. That's pretty optimistic considering that the average life span is eight years less than that.

American banks now hold nearly $2 trillion in first mortgages as collateral for what are considered the most stable loans in their portfolios. In addition, they hold nearly $80 billion in home equity loans above the first mortgages. These also are considered some of the "best" loans. Clearly American homeowners have transferred the wealth stored in their homes to the lenders. In this case, it leaves both in jeopardy. Given the wrong set of economic circumstances, the homeowners will default, leaving the banks with huge inventories of homes they can't sell.

CONSUMER DEBT

The rise in consumer debt over the last twenty years has been nothing less than phenomenal—from approximately $131 billion in 1970 to more than $794 billion in 1990! And the alarming fact about consumer debt is that it is available to virtually anyone and usually carries an annual finance charge of 18 percent and higher.

The Growth of Debt

Literally, Americans are working for the "company store" again. They labor at their jobs to pay the usurious interest they have come to accept as "normal." The increase in personal bankruptcies has grown at an alarming pace. In 1970 the total of personal bankruptcies was under 100,000. In 1980 it was 259,160, but by 1985 bankruptcies had risen to 312,000. In 1990 there were 685,439, and although official statistics are not available for 1991, the unofficial estimate is 900,000 plus. At the rate personal bankruptcies grew during the last decade, it is estimated that they will reach four million by the year 2000—and that's with no major economic crisis. This is not a problem. It is a symptom of a society awash in "easy money," which is what credit seems to be today. Eventually the majority of households will reach the stage where they cannot repay what they owe, nor will they be able to borrow more. At that point, the economy must stop while the debt is either repudiated (by a depression), devalued (by hyperinflation), or repaid (unthinkable).

It is the average income wage earner to whom the government will always turn when there is a need for more tax money. The quickest and least painful way (for the politicians) to raise money to keep the government operating is to create some new "revenue enhancements." Since tax increases are politically unpopular, the common method used is to initiate a tax bill designed to "soak the rich" and drop in a few revenue enhancers, such as eliminating the interest deduction for mortgages or the write-offs for contributions. There are several other possibilities, but these two will generate nearly $100 billion a year in new taxes by themselves. The unfortunate by-product of this action is to reduce the average consumer's level of spending. Therein lies the "Catch 22."

The increased tax revenues are offset by decreased spending. The decreased spending means fewer sales, which means fewer jobs, which means less revenue. . . .

BUSINESS DEBT

The trend in business debt is not as startling as that of the consumers, but it is equally disastrous. As of 1990, American businesses were paying out 7.7 percent of their gross incomes in interest alone—compared to 3.8 percent in 1970. Total business debt rose from $62 billion in 1970 to just over $700 billion in 1990. Much of this is debt on nonproductive capital, such as the junk bonds used for leveraged buy-outs during the eighties. Other companies that were not engaged in leveraged buy-outs took on considerable debt during this time in an effort to make their businesses less enticing to a buy-out. These were the so-called "poison pills" swallowed by so many companies. The leveraged buy-outs have ceased, but many of the poison pills are still around.

The debt burden of most businesses in America today is so great that virtually any slowdown in economic activity can place them in jeopardy. This was clearly demonstrated in the early stages of the 1990 recession when many major department store chains went under due to poor Christmas sales. These retailers had taken on so much debt that even a single slow season wiped them out. Some were chains that had been in operation for five decades or more. It was excessive debt that did them in; and it is excessive debt that will do in a great many more businesses in any prolonged downturn.

Government Debt

THE NATIONAL DEBT

The government has an income of approximately $1.4 trillion a year. It is spending approximately $1.8 trillion a year.

The total "on budget" debt of the government is $3.8 trillion as of late 1991; and the "off-budget" debt, which includes unfunded retirement liabilities, is another $2.5 trillion.

The only concern shown by most politicians is how to fund the deficits without changing the system or their own spending habits, which include incomes four times higher than the average workers they represent and a very generous retirement plan.

In the last several years a new "theory" has been developed in Washington that the national debt really doesn't matter since it is a smaller ratio of the country's gross national product (GNP) than it was thirty years ago. That is not true.

In 1980 the GNP was $2.7 trillion and the total debt was $914 billion—a ratio of 2.95 to 1. In 1990 the GNP was $5.4 trillion and the total debt was $3.8 trillion—a ratio of 1.42 to 1. Add to that figure the off-budget debt, and you get a better picture of the total. With a real national debt in excess of $6 trillion, the total debt is actually greater than the GNP. But even if it were not, the argument still makes no sense. The very fact that so much debt has been used in the economy inflates the GNP. For example: If housing contributes $1 trillion to the GNP, how much of that is inflation, created by excessive long-term financing?

The national debt has added to the GNP by virtue of inflation. If adjusted for inflation since 1980, the nation's GNP is actually $4.3 trillion.

In 1980 it took approximately 12 percent of the government's income to service its debt. To date, it requires approximately 18 percent (40 percent of all personal income taxes).

In 1980 the per capita indebtedness was approximately $4,000. Average median income (per family) was

$18,700—a ratio of 21 percent of annual income.

By 1990 the average indebtedness was approximately $15,000 per capita, with an average annual income of $30,000—a ratio of 50 percent of annual income! I would like someone to explain how the national debt doesn't really matter today.

FIGURES DON'T LIE

At the time of the Grace Commission's report in 1984, it estimated the total federal debt might reach $3 trillion by the year 2000. It exceeded that level in 1991.

All realistic estimates now place the potential debt at $13 to $20 trillion by the year 2000. That may sound distant to those of us who have lived most of our lives in the twentieth century, but it is less than ten years away.

At the current rate of growth, the federal deficits will feed approximately $7 trillion of additional debt into the economy between 1992 and the year 2000. There never has been anything approaching this level of debt funding in the history of mankind in so short a period of time, even on a percentage basis. The effects of this will be felt throughout the U.S.

and ultimately the world's economies. It is estimated that, at most, approximately $3 to $5 trillion is available from all sources to fund this deficit. That leaves only two logical conclusions: Either the government will take the necessary steps to control the budget and reduce the deficits drastically, or they will resort to monetizing (creating) the debt by printing massive amounts of new currency. How can they reduce this massive debt?

NECESSARY BUDGET CUTS

1. All federal payrolls would need to be reduced by approximately 40 percent. This would require the dismissal of 1.3 million employees, saving approximately $40 billion annually.

2. Welfare would need to be reduced by 25 percent, saving $46.5 billion annually.

3. Defense spending would need to be reduced by 25 percent, saving $10 billion annually. (This would require the closure of 3,000 obsolete military installations all across the country, resulting in the additional loss of 300,000 jobs in civilian-

related businesses.) It would also necessitate recalling at least one-half of all active U.S. military personnel stationed outside the United States.

4. Entitlement programs, such as student loans, farm support, education grants, and the myriad of other government-subsidized programs would need to be cut across the board by at least 25 percent, saving $60 billion.

As you can see, even with these cuts the budget has been reduced by only $146.5 billion a year. We would need to make another round of cuts to trim the additional $200 billion in actual overspending, if the government could not shift any spending to the off-budget category.

My obvious question is: Does anyone realistically believe that politicians are going to make the kinds of choices necessary to balance the budget? And would the average American be willing to make the sacrifices necessary to allow such cuts, even if the politicians wanted to do so?

Stress Signs

The following are presented as indicators signaling the excessive buildup of economic stress.

INDICATOR NUMBER 1:
THE SAVINGS AND LOAN COLLAPSE

The total effect on the economy of the Savings and Loan debacle has yet to be felt. Essentially it is two-fold: the immediate effect is a direct cost to the taxpayers of some $400 billion to cover the losses suffered by insured depositors.

By 1988 it was obvious that some major S&Ls were going to fail and would require a bailout by the government (taxpayers) to save the depositors' money. This sparked an investigation by the banking commission, which found a great many other S&Ls in trouble because of bad real estate loans.

In typical government fashion, they slammed the barn door after the horses had fled and clamped very tight regulations on the S&L industry. As a result, only a few S&Ls could meet the new guidelines for liabilities versus assets (equity). The primary reason they could not was that they had been operating under the previous looser requirements "suggested" by Washington. Using the authority of the regulatory commission, the government seized weak S&Ls and attempted to merge them with larger S&Ls. To do this the larger S&Ls, assuming the liabilities of smaller institutions, were given special tax incentives as well as promises of loans from the central bank.

During the Bush administration, the tax incentives were withdrawn (again retroactively), and even more stringent regulations were applied in an apparent attempt to placate screaming politicians who were bent on blaming somebody else. As a result, even larger numbers of S&Ls could not meet the new solvency requirements.

As soon as this information reached the public, there was a predictable reaction: panic. Once the panic began, the S&L industry was doomed.

INDICATOR NUMBER 2:
THE BANKS

For several years, keen-eyed accountants have been warning that some of the biggest banks in America were in financial trouble. Banks such as Chase Manhattan, New York City Bank, Bank of America, and dozens of others have been making loans that no prudent investor would ever have made with his own funds. Loans were made to Mexico, Brazil, Argentina, Yugoslavia, and Donald Trump—all of which were in trouble right from the beginning.

Depositors aren't especially watchful of the loans their banks are making, because their deposits are "protected" by a national insurance plan—the FDIC.

According to a 1990 audit done on the nation's banks, there are some 435 banks that are insolvent by *any* accounting standards. Among these are twenty of the largest banks, representing nearly $2 trillion in depositors' funds. Each dollar on deposit is a potential debt for the government if a bank fails. The FDIC is obligated to repay all depositors up to $100,000 per account.

In fact, so far the FDIC has covered *all* deposits, regardless of the amount. The reason is simple: the government fears that if any depositors lose money in a large bank's failure there could be a run on the deposits of other large banks that would spark a major bank collapse.

Many depositors are just finding out what the bankers have known for a decade or more: the FDIC itself is essentially broke. At its zenith, the insurance plan only had about 5 percent reserves for the funds it insured. In the late 1980s this amount declined to about 1.3 percent. When the final bill is due, the American taxpayers will be asked to pick up the tab (strictly off-budget, I'm sure).

INDICATOR NUMBER 3:
THE INSURANCE INDUSTRY

A great many insurance companies are in financial trouble—some because of imprudent investments in things like junk bonds but, over all, more are in trouble because of business and real estate loans they made when times were good.

According to the National Organization of Life and Health Insurance Guaranty Associations, 113 insurance companies were declared to be insolvent or impaired between 1988 and 1991, leaving millions of unpaid claims in their wake. Of course, most of these have been smaller companies. But Standard and Poor's Service, which rates all major insurance companies, is constantly downgrading the stability of some huge companies.

The profit margins in the insurance industry have declined as the companies have had to get more competitive. The growth of mutual funds and the onslaught of term insurance companies have pulled cash out of many of the lower-paying, whole-life plans. Also, many life insurance companies have branched out into the health insurance field and are facing rapidly declining margins of profit (or even large losses).

For decades, the whole-life (cash value) insurance companies, which represent the backbone of the industry, benefited from decreasing mortality rates as Americans lived longer. This helped the profit margins on older policies that were priced according to earlier mortality tables. These profits faded as increased competition forced most companies to adapt to the newer mortality tables and thus lower the costs of life insurance. Now many companies are looking at potentially devastating losses from early deaths due to the AIDS epidemic.

No one is suggesting that the insurance industry as a whole is insolvent. However, the next ten years are crucial as the big companies try to adjust to the declining real estate market and the impact that AIDS will have on our population. There will be many marginal insurance companies that will fail—leaving life, health, disability, and retirement annuities in default.

Since many businesses' retirement accounts are actually underwritten by insurance company annuities, this potentially will leave millions of people totally dependent on Social Security alone. I believe that is a risky dependency.

INDICATOR NUMBER 4: RETIREMENT ACCOUNTS

According to the Grace Commission's report, the Social Security system will need approximately $1.8 trillion a year to fund retirement and Medicare by the year 2000. Assuming a "normal" inflation rate of approximately 6 percent, the shortfall will be about $400 billion annually—in just nine years. Even if the government were saving the surpluses now, which it is not, the annual deficits would still run in excess of $300 billion.

Based on the need to further modify Social Security retirement, I believe it is quite possible that we will see the minimum retirement age raised to seventy before the end of this decade.

I also believe we will see Social Security taxes raised to 25 percent of gross wages, with no income cap. Basically, employers and employees will "voluntarily" contribute 25 percent of all earned income to the system. This will raise another $600 billion a year to feed both Social Security and the growing deficit. If the trust funds were intact, it is quite possible that the system would support the retirees who were born before 1938. By 2000 they will be sixty-two or older. For the rest of us, we will continue to work to provide the system with the money it will consume annually. By the year 2000 there will be only 3.2 workers for every retiree. In 1960 there were 14 workers for every retiree.

Although the federal government has not seen fit to store the surplus funds paid into the Social Security system, there is a large larder of funds available. It's called private retirement accounts.

There is approximately $600 billion stored in private IRAs. When the 401Ks, HR-10s, annuities, and the like are added to this, it is quite possible the total may reach $1.5 trillion. That great hoard of money will simply be too tempting for the politicians to pass up (in my opinion). It is very likely that private retirement accounts will ultimately be absorbed into the Social Security system and their owners given "equivalent" benefits.

It is also possible that before the need for retirement funds gets acute, the need for more spending in the economy will get larger. If so, the laws governing the use of retirement funds for education, buying homes, or even automobiles will be changed. If they are, I would suggest using those retirement account funds in place of current income to buy a home or educate your children. Then take your current income, pay the taxes, and store it for retirement. We are a long way from the confiscation of personal assets, but remember that tax-deferred funds are not yours: they are a gift from the government (at least in their thinking). The more indigestible (unable to absorb) you make your retirement funds, the safer they will be. Basically the Social Security system can't use your house, your cars, or your kids.

THE HEALTH CARE DEFICITS

The last area I want to discuss, in terms of deficits, is the huge black hole called "health care."

Both federal and state health care costs are escalating out of control. Medicare now costs more than $104 billion a year; up from $39 billion a decade ago. It is estimated (without the impact of AIDS) that federally supported health care costs will be more than $1.3 trillion by the year 2000.

When the costs of Medicaid (health services for the low-income families) are included, the total cost of government-provided health care represents nearly 30 percent of all taxes paid. Because of this and the escalating costs of private insurance, it seems certain that we will adopt some form of government-sponsored health insurance over the next few years. The thirty-four million Americans not covered by any kind of health insurance have virtually nowhere else to turn.

With only twelve cents of every government dollar allocated to meet needs actually reaching the recipient, it is a grossly inefficient system.

The only reasonable estimates I have been able to find on the potential costs of a government health insurance program that would cover all eligible Americans is approximately $180 billion a year (initially).

This represents additional spending above Medicare and Medicaid. Some cost reductions would be realized by the present system, so costs might drop by as much as $25 to $30 billion a year. What is the probable source of funding? Business taxes.

Unfortunately, what our government does not seem to grasp is that *businesses don't pay taxes.* They simply pass along the added costs to consumers. If the laws change to prohibit passing these costs along (as some politicians suggest), then the businesses will simply pack up and move to more amenable countries to make their products. Small businesses that cannot do this will end up in bankruptcy. Then we will lose the tax revenues they generate and add more people to the entitlements system.

AIDS

The cost of lifetime care for a

symptomatic AIDS patient is approximately $175,000 at the present time. Thus the care of ten AIDS patients represents a cost of $1,750,000; 100 patients represent a cost of $17,500,000; 1,000 patients represent a cost of $175,000,000. It is estimated that there will be at least 4 million symptomatic patients in the United States in this decade. Factor that cost into the national health care system, and the economic effects are catastrophic.

Deflation or Inflation?

THE DEFLATIONARY TREND

Several factors point toward a period of deflation in our economy.

First, we have just about pushed the limit on debt-funded housing. Over the past two decades home prices have escalated to the point that the average home buyer cannot afford to buy the average home. To provide the extra income needed to qualify for the more costly homes, many women made a mass exodus from their homes to the workplace during the seventies and eighties. But this has leveled off now, and a lot of women are opting to settle for less expensive houses so they can stay home with their children.

If this trend continues as expected, home prices should drop over the next few years or at least level out to some degree. This should result in a deflationary period for the second largest industry in our country. It will be good news for new buyers, but bad news for those using their homes as revolving lines of credit.

THE MECHANICS OF DEFLATION

The second deflationary factor occurs when prices exceed the ability of the average consumer to buy what is offered. Demand can be artificially stimulated by lowering interest rates until consumers are enticed to buy again, in which case they are buying based on the perceived value of the loan, *not* necessarily the product.

If allowed to run its full course, a deflationary spiral in the U.S. would wipe out millions of jobs. In a nation-wide deflation, there would be widespread unemployment.

However, because of the American consumer's addiction to credit, it is also quite possible that they will respond to yet another cycle of low interest rate stimuli by the government. If the Fed were to allow interest rates to drop to 6 percent or less, most Americans would respond by buying new cars, homes, boats, motorhomes, second homes, and other luxuries.

In my opinion, the recession of 1990-91 is not the signal of a major economic depression. I believe we have at least one more cycle left in our economy (possibly two) before we face the real test.

SCENARIO FOR THE 1990s

The mid-1990s may well yield a growth spurt during which an attempt will be made to outrun inflation. Such an action could easily spark hyperinflation. This philosophy would conform nicely with the previous patterns leading up to a major depression.

Assuming a three- or four-year period of stimulation (debt expansion) the stage would be set for another recession in the latter half of this decade. Depending on whether or not this downturn comes before or after an election year will greatly determine the response by the incumbent administration.

I will assume that the recession of 1990 "officially" ends by the first quarter of 1992—just in time for the presidential election. Bear in mind that even after a recession "officially" ends, the economy doesn't resume its former course as if nothing had ever happened. Many companies plan their work force at least a year in advance, so reductions in personnel may continue even after the economy recovers some steam. Also, retailers usually sell 20 percent or more of their yearly volume in December, so if they miss the Christmas season they will not expand again until the next season. Depending on the timing of a recovery, the statistical indicators may say a recession is over, but the average unemployed workers may not be able to tell the difference.

If my assumptions are accurate, by late 1992 or early 1993 the economy should be "perking" again, and since many of the previous three-year car notes will have been paid off (or the cars repossessed), the automobile companies should be looking at an improving economic situation.

Even with a reluctant president, 1993-1995 will probably be the era of massive new social programs, including (but not limited to) some form of national health care, low-income tax credits, subsidized day care, and whatever else the Congress can get past the president.

More Government Spending

I also assume the Democrats will concede the presidency for four more years but will concentrate on acquiring the votes to override the vetoes to their social programs. It is entirely possible we will see annual budget deficits in the *trillion* dollar range before this decade ends.

Once the economy has fully recovered from the recession, I rather suspect that our less-than-conservative politicians will sell the public on more debt to fund their social programs. I can already hear the politicians' appeals on the evening news. This should carry us well into the mid-nineties, with inflation becoming an increasingly nagging problem. I believe the price declines of the previous three or four years will be forgotten as inflation sparks again.

The single effective control for inflation is recession and, in a debt-run economy like ours, the primary retardant is higher interest rates. Almost certainly, higher interest rates will be employed in an attempt to control inflation.

It is my assumption that some event will initiate a massive spending cutback on the part of consumers. This could be a stock market crisis or an oil embargo, but more likely it will be the collapse of several "mega-banks," insurance companies, or large corporations.

There is no way to determine timing so far in advance. These events could occur in the mid-nineties or the latter part of this decade. It is always possible that some calamity could spark a panic at any time.

The Choices Ahead

POSITIVE STEPS TO RECOVERY

1. INITIATE SPENDING CUTS

If the Congress decides to follow the law as set down by the Gramm-Rudman Act and bring the federal budget into balance, you will know that the economy is headed down the path to recovery. Because of the enormity of the deficits, this will require across-the-board cuts in *every* budget area, including "entitlements." There is simply no way to bring the budget into balance and exclude 70 percent of current spending.

2. STOP THE "PORK BARREL" POLITICS

If the Congress allows the president a line-item veto so that he can reject specific areas of overspending without rejecting the entire budget, you will know it is serious about solving the problems.

As it is now, the Congress attaches hundreds of special-interest appropriation bills to the budget. The budget is usually associated with a politically sensitive issue such as civil rights or aid for dependent children. Then the politicians sit on the appropriations bill until midnight before the federal government's funds run out, sending it to the White House at the "twelfth" hour. The president is then confronted with either signing a budget that he doesn't agree with or shutting down the government and facing the wrath of angry citizens. If the politicians decide to stop this "pork barrel" method of funding their special projects, you'll know they are serious.

3. STOP THE DIVERSION OF NON-BUDGET FUNDS

If the president decides to stop robbing funds from Social Security and allow the budget to reflect the true deficits, including the off-budget entitlement programs, you will know the executive branch is also serious about solving the country's economic problem.

It is often too easy to blame the Congress for everything because it is the "big" spender. But the executive branch of our political system has pushed its pet projects too, including billion dollar airplanes with dubious performance and $500 hammers. When you see members of the White House staff driving their own cars to work and flying the commercial airlines like the rest of us, then you'll know the executive branch is serious too.

4. FORM A GOVERNMENT/BUSINESS PARTNERSHIP TO EXPAND EXPORTS

One economic factor that could signal an improving market for American goods is the expansion into eastern Europe by American businesses. This vast untapped market lacks the capital to buy many Western goods presently. But they will certainly emerge as a viable economic force before the end of this century, bringing 100 million new and willing consumers on line. This market base could enhance the U.S. economy to the point where we could absorb the present debt (assuming the politicians stop future waste). If the U.S. waits, we will find ourselves trying to catch up with the Asians in Europe, as we have in our own country.

NEGATIVE STEPS THAT CONTRIBUTE TO DECLINE

1. ADDITIONAL BORROWING TO FUND THE DEFICIT

Up to the time of this writing, our government has been able to avoid the consequences of hyperinflation because the annual deficits have been funded through loans.

The beginning of the real economic crisis in our country will come when the deficits reach the point where the funds cannot be raised through loans. Now nearly 20 percent of the annual deficit is funded by foreign investors, and almost $300 billion of the total national debt is owned directly by foreign investors. Perhaps as much as $600 billion is controlled through foreign-owned financial entities (banks, businesses, and the like).

Once the limit to which foreign investors will fund the U.S. debt is reached, a monetary crisis is not far off. Two factors can create this crisis. First, the foreign investors may see the U.S. government as a bad risk. That does not necessarily mean they believe the government is going under; it may just be that the value of the dollar is falling faster than the return on their investment.

The more money the government pulls out of the system to feed its own spending, the less that is available for businesses.

When the annual deficits (on budget and off) reach the level where the government can no longer fund them without taking critical operating funds away from industry, the economic blow-off is not far away.

2. MONETIZING THE DEBT

There is an urgent need for a federal law prohibiting the printing of additional currency to cover any budget shortfalls. Without such a law (carrying stiff penalties) there is little incentive to balance the budget.

The precedent is well established for the additional monetizing of our currency. Only this time it will be the printing of a currency already in circulation: the dollar. Simply put, we will eventually be forced to print what we can't borrow.

The current method of funding the government's debt is that the Treasury issues loan agreements (T-bills, bonds, and the like), which are sold through the federal reserve banks strategically located throughout the country.

In the event the Treasury decides to print fiat money to pay the government's bills, you can be sure the action will be cloaked in secrecy and disguised as something else, contrary to the securities' laws.

It should be noted here that the printing of money to pay the government's bills will be one of the last, and certainly the most desperate, measures because of the potential severity of the consequences.

3. INCREASE IN TAXES

Those who support a higher tax rate point out that not too long ago the maximum tax rate in our country was 70 percent and people still lived okay. What they miss is that most taxpayers didn't fall into the highest bracket and, in fact, the tax rate was designed specifically to encourage high income individuals to invest in the economy through the use of tax shelters.

Most certainly, average-income wage earners would balk at a tax rate of 50 percent or more, so it would need to be disguised. Allow me to share some creative ways to do this.

Gasoline tax. A federal gasoline tax would raise an additional $15 to $20 billion annually. Because of its impact on the lower income groups, a new tax on gasoline would probably provide some form of tax credit based on income.

Value-added tax. In the United States, no sales taxes are added until a product is sold to the consumer. Not so in the value-added system. Each recipient of raw materials or processed materials pays a tax. The raw materials sent to a processor are taxed. Then the processed materials are taxed to the manufacturer. They are taxed again when sold to the retailer. Another percentage is added when the products are sold to the consumers.

The value-added tax (on most products) can be as high as 40 percent when the totals are accumulated. Since the tax is paid by all classes of taxpayers, the income to the government is significantly greater than a graduated income tax.

A value-added tax on all goods and services in America could potentially add an additional $300 billion annually to the government's coffers. But it's important to remember that you don't get something for nothing. The $300 billion must be removed from the private sector economy to be given to the public sector. Doing so reduces the consumer's buying power and thus ripples through the entire economy.

A national lottery. Based on what the states are able to generate through their lotteries, a national lottery would net the government about $20 to $25 billion annually. If the government gets really creative and makes the proceeds tax free, the net could be as high as $100 billion.

The "success" of state lotteries in reducing taxes should forewarn everyone that lotteries *do not* reduce taxes. The net effect is an increase in income but at the cost of morality and more welfare to compensate for the money the poor spend on gambling.

So when you see an increase in taxes (other than a "soak the rich" tax) you know the politicians are desperate. The more visible the tax, such as the value-added tax, the more desperate they are for money. When they dip down into the pockets of the low-income groups through taxes on food, gasoline, and medicines, the end is nearing.

The Final Warnings

Mergers and buy-outs work only if the surviving entity is financially stronger than those absorbed. That was not true with the S&Ls, and it may not be true with the banks.

Larger banks do have access to the funds to buy out weaker institutions simply because of their size. But their debt-to-asset ratios are actually worse than many of the smaller banks. Unless there are some genuine efforts to bring the big banks under control, when the real economic crunch comes they will simply go under with a bigger bang.

We are witnessing the conversion of the entire banking industry into a new financial entity. If these mergers and acquisitions strengthen the banks, the economy will benefit. But if the big, shaky banks simply gobble up the smaller, more conservative banks to get at their asset base, it can be a critical blow to the economy.

The "merger mania" of the eighties left many businesses in shambles and helped to create the very crisis that now necessitates bank mergers. Watch very closely the ratings of these new "mega-banks."

Banks are private companies that make their money in the lending business. If the majority of their loans are participating (making their payments) then they are solvent. Once the number of bad loans exceeds the statistical number necessary to repay the depositors' interest, the bank will fail without government intervention.

In a bad economy with unemployment exceeding 10 percent or more, many of the normally sound loans will default. This crack in the economy will be highly publicized because it will swallow up hundreds of banks, large and small, and will require a *trillion dollars* or more in additional government subsidies.

Where will the funds come from at a time when the economy is flagging and the government's income is declining? The same three options are available: new taxes, more loans, or printed money.

BUSINESS FAILURES AND DEPARTURES

The single bright spot that I can see on the horizon is the ability of American entrepreneurs to adapt to virtually any situation and still make a profit.

The biggest negative is the excessive burden placed on them by our political system.

When the additional factors of mandatory health insurance, workmen's compensation, liability insurance, property taxes, inventory taxes and, eventually, value-added taxes are dumped on small and medium-sized businesses, we will see some massive failures.

The interdependent relationships between banks and businesses tend to feed each other. If one goes, the other is sure to follow.

As banks fail, the primary source of operating capital dries up for the local businesses. Then, as businesses fail, other banks are jeopardized because they have loaned to businesses that are dependent on the failed enterprises.

OUR NATION TURNING AWAY
FROM BIBLICAL PRINCIPLES

In Deuteronomy 28:12-13 God makes His people a promise: ''The Lord will open for you His good storehouse, the heavens, to give rain to your land in its season and to bless all the work of your hand; and you shall lend to many nations, but you shall not borrow. And the Lord shall make you the head and not the tail, and you only shall be above, and you shall not be underneath, if you will listen to the commandments of the Lord your God, which I charge you today, to observe them carefully.''

Then in Deuteronomy 28:43-45 another sobering promise is made: ''The alien who is among you shall rise above you higher and higher, but you shall go down lower and lower. He shall lend to you, but you shall not lend to him; he shall be the head, and you shall be the tail. So all these curses shall come on you and pursue you and overtake you until you are destroyed, because you would not obey the Lord your God by keeping His commandments and His statutes which He commanded you.''

Just as I believe our material wealth is a by-product of observing

God's commandments and following His directions, so I believe the present state of our economy is an indication of violating basic biblical principles provided in the Bible.

What Can You Do?

What it really boils down to is this:

1. Many Christians will suffer needlessly because of their own foolish decisions and failure to plan properly, based on God's Word.

2. Others will suffer through no fault of their own simply because God wants to use them as examples of steadfastness in the face of adversity.

3. There will be some Christians who will experience God's supernatural provision—mentally, financially, physically, and spiritually.

Psalm 50, verses 14 and 15, are some of my most cherished Scriptures. "Offer to God a sacrifice of thanksgiving, and pay your vows to the Most High; and call upon Me in the day of trouble; I shall rescue you, and you will honor Me."

GET OUT OF DEBT

Recently I wrote a book entitled *Debt-Free Living*. In it I tried to discuss all the arguments for and against borrowing in our economy, so I won't expound on that material here. However, I believe there are some pertinent points that must be made in relation to the coming crisis in our economy.

First, debt created this problem, and debt will make it far worse before we see any resolution. Debt is not the problem though; debt is merely the mechanism by which weak-willed politicians feed their constituents easy money—which is what borrowed money is. Debt, therefore, has allowed the government to spend money it didn't have on projects that most Americans wouldn't have approved if they had been required to pay for them with tax dollars.

Second, there is no way to sustain debt spending for an indefinite period of time. Eventually the interest accumulation will exceed anyone's (or any country's) ability to keep the debt current.

Let me restate an absolute principle of economics: No one, government or otherwise, can spend more than he makes indefinitely. At some point the compounding interest will consume all the money in the world. We might disagree about *when* the end will come, but not *if*.

Currently, if you take an early withdrawal on a retirement account, you will have to pay additional taxes and a penalty for early withdrawal (for those under the age of 59½). Even so, it still makes economic sense to take the penalty and pay the taxes just to know your home is debt-free. If you can't pay your real estate taxes in a bad economy, you can lose your home in three years (in most states). However, if you can't pay the mortgage payments you can lose it in three months.

You need to look at every loan you make from this point on to determine what the contingent liabilities are. If you are obligated beyond the assigned collateral, don't borrow! If you already have loans where you are in surety, do everything possible (within reason) to retire the outstanding loans and avoid any future surety.

Set as a goal to be debt-free as soon as possible. When the economy recovers, and it will, don't change your mind because things are looking better.

Plan for Retirement

If you weigh the alternatives of either starting a retirement plan while paying off your home or using the retirement funds to pay your home off early and then starting the retirement plan, there is no contest. Assuming you have at least twenty years before retirement, you will do much better financially by paying the mortgage off first. It's the simple concept of compounding interest working for you rather than against you.

If you are within ten years of retirement, or are retired already, I would suggest some radical changes in your perspective.

For those with sizable assets ($250,000 or more) I suggest that you follow Solomon's advice and diversify as rapidly as the economy will allow. "Divide your portion to seven, or even to eight, for you do not know what misfortune may occur on the earth" (Ecclesiastes 11:2).

You need to look at investing in some assets outside the United States through quality mutual funds and other instruments that have sound track records. The certainty is that the whole world's economy will not fail. Some countries will benefit, while others will suffer. The difficulty is in determining which will benefit and which will not. The best "hedge" is to diversify as much as possible—not only in different areas of the economy, but also in different areas of the world. For instance, don't keep all of your assets in California real estate, even if it has always done well for you. We have not had a major economic tremor in the last fifty years, much less a calamity.

The one caution I would give is don't be panicked into making foolish investments by following the advice of those who profit from fear. More often than not these are the "gold bugs." They would have everyone place a large amount of his assets in gold or silver as protection against the big collapse.

I might put a lot more confidence in their suggestions if someone other than a gold salesman would substantiate their confidence in precious metals. There is no doubt that our economy would be better off today if we had remained on the gold standard. But we have been divorced from it for more than fifty years now. In my opinion, neither the United States nor any other major economic power will return to the gold standard in our lifetimes. To do so would require that gold be revalued to approximately $64,000 an ounce. It is far more likely that we will evolve into a totally cash-less economy as a result of the coming crisis, not one based on precious metals.

For those with lesser assets and less flexibility with their retirement assets I would suggest two things: First, seek some alternative vocational training during the interval between the next upswing in the economy and the calamity that appears to be coming. Any investment can be lost, no matter how secure it appears at present. But vocational skills will last for as long as you live and will be marketable regardless of the economy.

It is important to understand that not everyone will be mired down economically in a depression (or even in hyperinflation). Many people will actually prosper during this period as they have the resources to take advantage of the opportunities presented. This group will have the assets to pay for the services they need. So take a course in plumbing, electricity, carpentry, cabinetmaking, computer science, or anything else that is marketable. Determine what your basic aptitudes are and exploit them to the highest degree possible. If you can become highly proficient at any one thing, rarely will you be without a source of income.

The second suggestion is to diversify even with limited assets. You may not be able to buy land in Poland or Yugoslavia, but you can invest in a good international mutual fund. If your assets are invested too narrowly, your risk is multiplied. Remember that the goal is not necessarily to maximize your return as much as it is to minimize your losses.

If you are retired, out of debt, and have some surplus money, in a deflationary economy your dollars will stretch farther. But if you're retired, living on a fixed income with limited assets, and hit a hyperinflationary cycle, your life savings can be consumed in a startlingly short amount of time. So it is important not to get stuck in a no-risk mentality about investing. Treasury bonds may be great in a stable or deflationary economy because they are virtually risk free. But if you believe any of the suppositions I have presented on hyperinflation might come true, you would do well to place some of your retirement assets in investments such as growth mutual funds and international funds.

They won't do well during a deflationary cycle, but they will keep pace with the economy in an inflationary period.

What happens if the government decides to absorb your retirement funds into the Social Security system? Then you simply say that you have done the best you could with what you had and go back to work again. In the meantime I would not put all my surplus into a retirement account, even if I could. In the highest tax bracket you still pay only 33 percent of your earnings in federal income taxes (at present). The after-tax surplus can be invested in tax-deferred investments, such as annuities totally outside the retirement system. Based on the past actions of our government, I believe it is worth paying the taxes and controlling at least some of your savings.

One additional thing you can do is write and call your elected officials to get their official positions on the theft of funds from the Social Security Trust. If they won't take a public stand against this, make it a campaign issue during the next election. You would be amazed how agreeable many politicians are during an elec-

tion period. The greatest asset we
have as voters is public awareness.

GET INVOLVED IN
THE POLITICAL PROCESS

I am amazed how few people
ever get involved in the political process. They have been brainwashed
into believing that their voices don't
really count; believe me they do.

I had a senator tell me that as
few as two hundred calls or letters
for or against a particular bill will often sway his vote. He also added that
many of his colleagues have voiced
the same comment.

We have allowed the political
process to create a new caste system,
with our elected officials serving like
a collective monarchy. They pass
laws restricting the rights and free-
doms for the majority of Americans,
while exempting themselves from
the process.

I doubt that many voters know
the Congress has exempted itself
from all the civil rights and anti-dis-
crimination laws passed. It has exempted itself from our retirement
system, our school system, and even
the normal day-care system.

Why should we think that our governmental leaders would suddenly get conservative when it comes to running our nation's economy? We have surrendered control of our finances to a group of people ignorant in basic economics. It is time that the average American woke up and realized that a housewife who has learned to live on an average income is eminently more qualified to make economic decisions than is the average politician.

This is not a philosophical or even a political issue. It is our future we're discussing, and if we don't make some dramatic changes, it is just a matter of time before the economy fails. Keep in mind that the people who are trying to convince us that an economic crisis will not occur are the same ones who spend $500 for hammers that are commercially available for $12, buy 20¢ bolts for $60, spend $40 billion a year in taxpayers' funds not to grow food, and increase the welfare rolls from 6 million to 14 million people while spending $3 trillion to accomplish this remarkable task.

The list of abuses could go on and on. The point is, the next time you think that you may not be qualified to counsel the politicians on how the economy should be run, consider whether or not you would pay annual bonuses to the post office administrators who operate the postal system in the red each and every year.

If you don't want your children and grandchildren to live in a third-rate country with fewer jobs and total dependency on foreign goods and money, you *need* to get involved.

As Harry Figgie accurately stated, "This is not a Republican or a Democratic problem. It is an American problem."

I see politicians chiding the "wealthy" and then voting salaries for themselves that place them in the top 5 percent of incomes in America. I see honest small business people struggling to survive under the heavy burden of taxes, insurance, and foreign competition. Our political system makes us especially vulnerable to outside competition because our government gives benefits to our competitors while penalizing American companies. It would seem the basic philosophy of our government is help your enemies and hurt your friends. The Japanese, for instance, consider their entrepreneurs as a national resource and do everything possible to preserve and protect them—even creating special legislation in order to make them more competitive.

We do the exact opposite. President Calvin Coolidge once said, "The chief business of American people is business." Our present herd of politicians no longer accepts that doctrine. Their philosophy is "The business of America is politics." Unfortunately they have been quite successful in convincing Americans that the economy runs to serve the political system.

This constant and growing drain on our resources strips the business community of the vital capital needed to create more jobs and compete with countries that take our innovations and sell them back to us.

Allow me to outline a few specific suggestions that you can use when contacting your senators and congressmen.

1. *Demand that the Congress and the president abide by the Gramm-Rudman Act and balance the national budget—immediately.*

I would further demand that *all* spending programs be included in the law—no exceptions. Until and unless all spending is included "in-budget" the law will not work. It is very much like the wage and price controls we discussed earlier; the exceptions quickly become the norm.

What happens in the Washington political system is a process called "trade-offs." In this process those who want something trade a favor for a favor. The result is usually legislation that is good for their district but bad for the country. The only way to avoid this (if at all) is to require all programs to be cut by the same percentage and to allow line-item vetoes so that so-called "pork barrel" spending is not attached to nonrelated legislation.

2. Keep track of how the politicians in your area vote on spending bills.

The group known as Citizens Against Government Waste watches this area carefully and publishes a quarterly report. I can assure you that if you come to an election meeting armed with specific facts about how your representatives voted to use tax-payers' money, they will think about the bills they back the next time they vote in Washington.

The number for the Citizens Against Government Waste is 1-800-USA-DEBT, and the address is 1301

Connecticut Avenue, NW, Suite 400, Washington, DC 20036.

3. *Every chance you get, challenge the mentality that all business people and the profits they generate are somehow inherently evil. That is total nonsense and merely a method of "scapegoating."*

Instead, begin to prompt your elected officials to use the system to promote more competitive enterprises. I personally would like to see the government allow tax-free return on investments made to businesses that compete directly with foreign imports.

In reality we would be losing very few tax dollars since these are industries where we are no longer competitive anyway. And for every tax dollar lost, it has been shown that we would gain nearly $1,000 in taxable revenue.

It is a national disgrace that Americans invented the multivalve car engine, video recorders, color television, digital electronics, computer-controlled machines, and so on, but are no longer competitive in any of these industries.

4. *Check out the curriculum being taught in your local schools and see*

if it is anti-free-market biased. It would shock most Americans to realize that a great deal of the economic information being fed their children in grammar schools, high schools, and especially state universities is blatantly socialistic, if not openly communistic.

If we continue to take handouts from the government, how can we speak out against government waste? To take a stand against waste means that God's people must also refuse to take FHA or VA loans. Christian farmers need to say, "Thanks, but no thanks, Uncle." Churches need to take care of their own poor, rather than expecting welfare or Medicare to do so.

In short, it means "walking our talk." James said in his letter: "But prove yourselves doers of the word, and not merely hearers who delude themselves" (James 1:22).

If I am wrong and you do all the things I have suggested, the worst that can happen is that you will end up out of debt and be more involved with our political system.

If I am right and you do nothing, you'll end up losing everything you own and be totally dependent on the very system that created the mess we are facing.

Keep in mind that God has everything under control. You can do your part by giving sacrificially to the Lord's work; if you do, you cannot lose. "Because of the proof given by this ministry they will glorify God for your obedience to your confession of the gospel of Christ, and for the liberality of your contribution to them and to all" (2 Corinthians 9:13).

Just as the day of the Lord will come as a thief in the night, so an economic collapse will come in the midst of what appears to be economic prosperity. The very debt that creates the prosperity ultimately destroys it.

If you truly surrender your finances to God, you will experience His faithfulness. I pray the Lord will give you the wisdom to do as He directs you.

For a much more comprehensive treatment of an impending collapse of our U.S. economy, please see my latest book, *The Coming Economic Earthquake.*

What Can You Do?

Other Materials by Larry Burkett:

Books in This series:

Financial Freedom
Sound Investments
Major Purchases
Insurance Plans
Giving and Tithing
Personal Finances
Surviving the 90's Economy
Your Financial Future

Other Books:

The Coming Economic Earthquake
Debt-Free Living
Financial Planning Workbook
How to Manage Your Money
Using Your Money Wisely
Your Finances in Changing Times
New Book on Retirement Planning
(hardcover release coming
in October 1992)

Videos:

Your Finances in Changing Times
Two Masters
How to Manage Your Money
The Financial Planning Workbook

Other Resources:

Financial Planning Organizer
Debt-Free Living Cassette